To

From

For Isabella, Emilia and Rory, and Francesca
and Lawrence, who all appear in this book
A.L.

Written and compiled by Sophie Piper
Illustrations copyright © 2009 Anthony Lewis
This edition copyright © 2009 Lion Hudson

The moral rights of the author and illustrator have
been asserted

A Lion Children's Book
an imprint of
Lion Hudson plc
Wilkinson House, Jordan Hill Road,
Oxford OX2 8DR, England
www.lionhudson.com
UK ISBN 978-0-7459-6147-7
US ISBN 978-0-8254-7898-7

First edition 2009
This printing September 2009
10 9 8 7 6 5 4 3 2 1

Acknowledgments
All unattributed prayers are by Sophie Piper and
Lois Rock, copyright © Lion Hudson.

Bible extracts are taken or adapted from the *Good
News Bible*, published by The Bible Societies/
HarperCollins Publishers Ltd, UK © American
Bible Society 1966, 1971, 1976, 1992.

The Lord's Prayer (on page 75) from *Common
Worship: Services and Prayers for the Church of England*
(Church House Publishing, 2000) is copyright ©
The English Language Liturgical Consultation, 1988
and is reproduced by permission of the publishers.

Prayer by Mother Teresa (on page 46) used by
permission.

A catalogue record for this book
is available from the British Library

Typeset in 18/22 Goudy Old Style BT
Printed and bound in China
by Printplus Ltd

Distributed by:
UK: Marston Book Services Ltd, PO Box 269,
Abingdon, Oxon OX14 4YN
USA: Trafalgar Square Publishing, 814 N Franklin
Street, Chicago, IL 60610
USA Christian Market: Kregel Publications, PO Box
2607, Grand Rapids, MI 49501

The Lion Book of
PRAYERS
To
Read & Know

WRITTEN AND COMPILED BY SOPHIE PIPER

ILLUSTRATED BY ANTHONY LEWIS

LION
CHILDREN'S

Contents

Praising the Maker God

In the beginning, says the Bible, there was nothing –
except God.

God spoke, and called the whole world into being.
And God's world was good. Very good.

God made the sky and
the birds that fly in it.

God made the mountains
and the plains and the many
kinds of plants that grow.

God made
animals for all the
different habitats
of the world.

6

God made the sun that shines in the daytime and the moon and stars that shine in the night.

God made the sea and all the creatures that live in it.

God made people – man and woman to take care of the world.

7

A psalm of praise

Praise the Lord from heaven,
all beings of the height!
Praise him, holy angels
and golden sun so bright.

Praise him, silver moonlight,
praise him, every star!
Let your praises shine
throughout the universe so far.

Praise the Lord from earth below,
all beings of the deep!
Lightning, flash! You thunder, roar!
You ocean creatures, leap.

Praise him, hill and mountain!
Praise him, seed and tree.
Praise him, all you creatures
that run the wide world free.

Let the mighty praise him.
Let the children sing.
Men and women, young and old:
Praise your God and king.

From Psalm 148

In praise of God's majesty

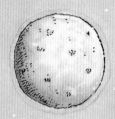

The sunrise
tells of God's glory;
the moonrise
tells of God's glory;
the starshine
tells of God's glory;
the heavens
tell of God's glory.

Based on Psalm 19

Our Lord and God! You are worthy to
   receive glory, honour and power.
For you created all things,
and by your will they were given
   existence and life.

Revelation 4:11

O God,
You are more splendid than the lights that
   shine across the universe.
You are more powerful than forces that
   scatter the stars.
You whisper to me more gently than the
   night-time breeze.
Your blessings are as sure as the sunrise.

In praise of God's goodness

I praise the Lord with all my soul,
my strength, my heart, my mind:
he blesses me with love and grace
and is for ever kind.

Based on Psalm 103:1–4

Dear God,
When everything is going wrong,
I sometimes wonder why you let bad
things happen.

But then you open my eyes to the
majesty of your world, and I know once
more that you are far greater than I
can imagine, and I believe once more
that your love and goodness will not be
overcome.

Based on the book of Job

Praise the Lord with trumpets
all praise to him belongs;
praise him with your music
your dancing and your songs!

Based on Psalm 150

A world of praise

Bless the Lord of heaven above,
sing to God with thanks and love.

Praise him for the joyful spring,
bringing life to everything.

Praise him for the blossom trees,
birds and butterflies and bees.

Praise him for the cloud and rain,
and for sunshine once again.

Bless the Lord of heaven above,
sing to God with thanks and love.

Praise him, all you fishes in the sea!
Praise him, all you birds that fly above!
Praise him, all you creatures in the whole wide world!
God is love! God is love!

Thanksgiving

God made the world and everything in it, says the Bible. It is right for people to give God thanks for all the things they have and for God's love and care in good times and in bad times.

God sends the rain
that makes the grass
grow in the pastures.

God has promised
summer and winter,
seedtime and harvest
for ever.

God sends the sun that
ripens the crops in gardens,
fields and orchards.

For God's love

Give thanks to the Lord, because he is good;
his love is everlasting.
He alone performs great miracles;
his love is everlasting.
By his wisdom he made the heavens;
his love is everlasting.
He built the earth on the deep waters;
his love is everlasting.
Give thanks to the God of heaven;
his love is everlasting.

From Psalm 136:1, 4–6

Thank you, great Maker God,
that in your great wide world
you made a space for me.

Thank you, great Maker God,
that I am as I am –
a part of your wide world.

For family and friends

Thank you, dear God,
for putting me in a family that is held together
  with love.

Thank you, dear God, for the little
place that is my home – more special
to me than all the stars in the universe.

Thank you, dear God,
for the blessing of things that stay the same:
for people we have known for ever
and the familiar paths where we walk.

Thank you, dear God,
for the blessing of things that change:
for newcomers with their new customs,
new ways of doing things, new paths
    to discover.

Thank you, dear God,
for the blessing of the old and the blessing
    of the new.

For a wonderful world

Dear God,
Thank you for the earth that holds us up,
and gravity that holds us down.

Thank you for the little things
we notice every day
that shine on earth
with heaven's gold
and cheer us on our way.

Thank you, God, for birds that sing
from high up in the trees;
thank you for the butterflies
that dance upon the breeze.
Thank you for the wild beasts
of every stripe and hue.
Thank you for the whole round globe
of green and gold and blue.

Thank you, God, for lobsters
and the strange things of the sea.
Thank you for the insects –
the mosquito and the flea.
Thank you for the frogs and toads,
and bright-eyed things that lurk
among the ooze and mud and slime
and long-neglected murk.

For food and harvest

Let us take a moment
To thank God for our food,
For friends around the table
And everything that's good.

For all the harvests of the world:
we give you thanks, O God.
For those who work to gather the crops:
we give you thanks, O God.
For those who fill our shops with food:
we give you thanks, O God.
For food to eat and food to share:
we give you thanks, O God.

The harvest of our garden
is astonishingly small;
but oh, dear God, we thank you
that there's anything at all.

Morning is here,
The board is spread,
Thanks be to God,
Who gives us bread.

Anonymous

For all I have

Thank you, God in heaven,
For a day begun.
Thank you for the breezes,
Thank you for the sun.
For this time of gladness,
For our work and play,
Thank you, God in heaven,
For another day.

Traditional

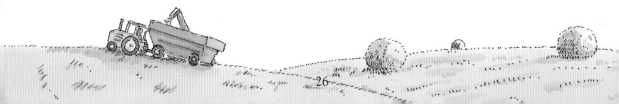

Thank you, God,
for eyes and seeing;
for ears and hearing;
for a nose and smelling;
for a tongue and tasting;
for skin and feeling;
thank you for my body:
my passport to the world.

Dear God,
Thank you for the things I have in abundance,
to enjoy with frivolity.

Thank you for the things of which I have enough,
to enjoy thoughtfully.

Thank you for the things that I lack
that keep me trusting in your many blessings.

Forgiving and forgiven

To know God's love, says the Bible, people must live in the way that is good and right.

That means being ready to admit when they have done wrong. It means forgiving others.

Jesus said this:

'If you forgive others the wrongs they have done to you, your Father in heaven will also forgive you.'

Matthew 6:14

Not hitting back can end a fight.

Gentle words can end an angry quarrel.

To forgive is to begin to put things right.

People who are kind and friendly make the world more fun.

Saying sorry

Dear God,
For the silly things I have done wrong
I am sorry.

For the serious things I have done wrong
I am sorry.

For the things I didn't even know were wrong
I am sorry.

For all the things I need to put right
Make me strong.

The wrong I have done
now makes me sad;

The love that God gives
will make me glad.

God, have pity on me, a sinner!

From Jesus' parable of the Pharisee and the tax collector, Luke 18:13

Dear God,
The lies I told have grown like brambles,
and now I am trapped in a tangle of thorns.

Dear God, I don't know what to do; I just
want to be free again to tell the truth.

Making amends

Dear God,
Sometimes, when I do wrong,
I can help put things right.
I might need to say something.
I might need to do something.
I might need to pay for something.
May I be ready to do what I can.

Sometimes, when I do wrong,
I cannot repair the damage.
Not with words.
Not with deeds.
Not with money.

Please bring hope where I have caused sadness.
Please bring healing when I have caused hurt.

Mending things
is so much better
than ending things.

I will get up
and go to the person I have wronged
and I will say this:
'I am sorry for what I did.
'I don't deserve for you to like me,
but I would like to make things better.'

A prayer inspired by the words of the prodigal son, Luke 15:21

Forgiving others

Dear Jesus,
  I find it hard to love my enemies.
    I do not want to pray for those who
      are cruel to me.

        I want to follow you,
          but you are walking far
            ahead of me.
            Please come and take
            me by the hand.

Based on Matthew 5:43–48

Dear God,
I am not ready to forgive
but I am ready to be made ready.

How to forgive:

Take one grudge
and drop it in the deep pond
of faith in God's love.
Wait a while.

Each grudge has a hard shell of anger.
With love and faith it will soften.
From within, the seed of forgiveness will sprout
and grow into the tree of peace.

A new beginning

God says this:
Do not cling onto what happened in the past.
Watch for the new thing I am going to do.
I will make a path through the wilderness
and those who travel on it will be joyful again.

A prayer inspired by the words of the prophet,
Isaiah 43:18–21

Take my wrongdoing
and throw it away,
down in the deep of the sea;
welcome me into your kingdom of love
for all of eternity.

Based on Micah 7:18–20

God has baptized the day
in the dark waters of night;
and now it rises clean and shining,
bright with the gold light of heaven.

May I step bravely into this new day,
determined to walk the way of goodness,
  as God's child
under God's heaven.

Choosing the right way

Life offers so many choices, says the Bible, but there is only one thing that matters.

People should respect God and God's commandments. That is what human beings were created to do.

One day, everything they have done will be judged in the light of God's love and goodness.

Those who say they love God must love and welcome one another.

In God's family, everyone is of equal value.

Small deeds of kindness are part of living as God wants.

God's good laws

֍

Come, my young friends, and listen to me,
and I will teach you to honour the Lord.
Would you like to enjoy life?
Do you want long life and happiness?
Then hold back from speaking evil
and from telling lies.
Turn away from evil and do good;
strive for peace with all your heart.

Psalm 34:11–14

Trust in the Lord and do good.

Psalm 37:3

Do not follow the advice
  of the wicked,
but obey every word of God.

For the wicked are nothing more
than wisps of straw in the autumn
gale; but the righteous are like trees
that grow by the lifegiving river, bearing
leaves and fruit in their season.

From Psalm 1

O God,
Your word is a lamp to guide me
and a light for my path.

Psalm 119:105

Ten great commandments

෨

O Lord,
I have heard your laws.
May I worship you.
May I worship you alone.
May all I say and do show respect for your holy name.
May I honour the weekly day of rest.
May I show respect for my parents.
May I reject violence so that I never take a life.
May I learn to be loyal in friendship and so learn to be faithful in marriage.
May I not steal what belongs to others.
May I not tell lies to destroy another person's reputation.
May I not be envious of what others have, but may I learn to be content with the good things you give me.

A prayer based on the Ten Commandments, Exodus 20

Everyday wisdom

O God,
Make me good.
Make me wise.
Make me hardworking.
Make me honest.
Make me tactful.
Make me generous.
Make me truthful.
Make me loyal.
But most of all,
dear God,
make me your child.

Based on Proverbs

May my life shine
like a star in the night,
filling my world
with goodness and light.

From Philippians 2:15

I pray for the person I see in the mirror,
who's really a lot like me;
who needs to grow older and wiser and kinder
to be the best they can be.

Dear God,
I resolve this day to do
    what is right,
even if no one else will
    join me.

When I have to choose
between right and wrong,
help me make the right choice
and give me peace in my heart.

From Colossians 3:15

Faith, hope and love

We can do no great things,
Only small things with great love.

Mother Teresa of Calcutta (1910–97)

Help me, Lord, to show your love.

Help me to be patient and kind, not jealous or conceited or proud. May I never be ill-mannered, selfish or irritable; may I be quick to forgive and forget.

May I not gloat over wrongdoing, but rather be glad about things that are good and true.

May I never give up loving: may my faith and hope and patience never come to an end.

Based on 1 Corinthians 13:4–7

Believe in yourself and think well of others;
Believe in others and show them your love;
Believe in the greatness beyond all knowing:
Within and beyond, below and above.

God's spirit within

Let the Spirit come
like the winds that blow:
take away my doubts;
help my faith to grow.

Let the Spirit come
like a flame of gold:
warm my soul within;
make me strong and bold.

Spirit of God
put love in my life.
Spirit of God
put joy in my life.
Spirit of God
put peace in my life.

Spirit of God
make me patient.
Spirit of God
make me kind.
Spirit of God
make me good.

Spirit of God
give me faithfulness.
Spirit of God
give me humility.
Spirit of God
give me self-control.

From Galatians 5:22–23

BOOKMOBILE
101 RAGGED EDGE ROAD SOUTH
CHAMBERSBURG, PA 17202

49

Praying for one another

Those who want to live as God's friends, says the Bible, must never give up praying.

They should stay alert as they pray, and give thanks to God.

They should pray for other people, asking God to help them. In this way, God's kingdom of love and goodness will grow.

It is good to help one another.

It is good to remember those who are sad.

It is good to pray
for others.

It is good to be aware
of people in need.

It is good to be
a loyal friend.

For family

Dear God, bless all my family
as I tell you each name;
and please bless each one differently
for no one's quite the same.

God bless Grandad
through the bright blue day.
God bless Grandad
through the dark grey night.
God bless Grandad
when we hug together.
God bless Grandad
when we're out of sight.

Dear God,
I want to pray for what my dad would pray for
if he wasn't so busy.

I want to pray for what my mum would pray for
if she wasn't so tired.

I want to pray for what my brother would pray for
if he wasn't glued to the screen.

I want to pray for what my sister would pray for
if she wasn't dancing to music.

These are my prayers, dear God;
will you please tell me the words.

For friends

May the things I say
help to build trust and friendship.

May the things I do
help to build trust and friendship.

May I set my heart
to build trust and friendship.

Dear God,
May everyone I meet
in school know they
can count on me to
be kind.

O God,
Help us to forgive our friends
when they let us down.

Dear God,
Help me to make good friends
who make it easy for me to be a good person.
Help me to walk away from bad friends
who make it easy for me to be a bad person.
Help me to be a good friend
who makes it easy for others to be good.

For those who are sad

God is our shelter and strength,
always ready to help in times of trouble.
So we will not be afraid, even if the earth is shaken
and mountains fall into the ocean depths;
even if the seas roar and rage,
and the hills are shaken.

Psalm 46:1–3

When you walk in darkness
may the stars shine for you.

When you walk in sadness
may the angels sing for you.

When you walk in sorrow
may the God of love bless you.

Help us not to worry, dear God.
Remind us to ask you for the things we need
and give thanks.

Give us the peace that comes from knowing that all
our worries are safe with you.

From Philippians 4:6–7

For those who are grieving

O God,
Put an end to death.
Put an end to grief and crying and pain.
Make all things new.
Lead us to heaven.

From Revelation 21

Lead us through the darkness
where we cannot see our way;
make a path for us to walk
into the light of day.

The autumn leaves were laid to rest
But now the trees are green,
And signs that God brings all to life
Throughout the world are seen.

And Jesus is alive, they say,
And death is not the end.
We rise again in heaven's light
With Jesus as our friend.

For all the world

What does God want people to do?

The Bible says that God made a beautiful world that would provide people with all they needed. The job of humankind is to take care of it.

The Bible also says that God wants everyone to enjoy freedom, justice and peace. Those who love God should do all they can to make these things real. They should care about those who are poor, those who are hungry and those who have no place to call home.

Everyone deserves clean drinking water.

Everyone deserves a chance to make the best of their life.

Everyone deserves a place to call home.

Everyone deserves enough to eat.

Planet earth

∽

We think the earth is ours.

We dig it, drill it, plough it, mine it, pave it.

Then, from within the heart of things, the earth erupts. It shakes, it quakes, it shifts, it drifts.

May we learn to respect the earth, for it is shaped by forces greater than our own, and we should live in awe of them.

The winter brook flows quick and green
with swirling eddies in between
its tiny falls of sparkling spray
that curl and ripple on their way.

The summer brook is slow and grey
and choked with all we've thrown away:
old cans and bags and battered shoes
and things that we no longer use.

God our Maker, send the rain
to wash the whole world clean again.
Then teach us to respect and care
for fire, water, earth and air.

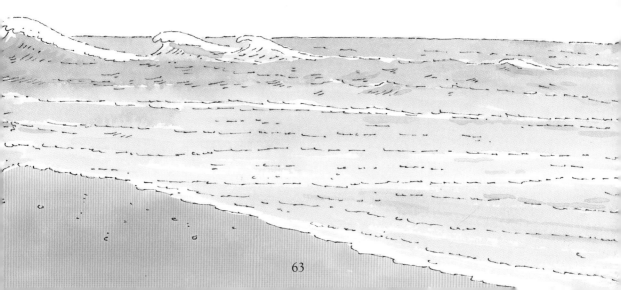

All God's creatures

Have you heard the choir of all God's creatures –
the operatic whale

      and the slightly off-key buffalo;
      the timid, squeaky-voiced mouse
    and the clear carolling of the blackbird?

   Listen carefully:
listen for the high notes and the low notes,
for the solo and the chorus,
for the melody and the rhythm,
for the songs of life in all its variety.

Leave space for the creatures to go on living.
Leave space for the creatures to go on singing.
Leave space for the song of all creation
in praise of the creator.

He prayeth best, who loveth best
All things both great and small;
For the dear God who loveth us,
He made and loveth all.

S. T. Coleridge (1772–1834)

Bless our little garden. May it be a safe place for all the little creatures that creep and scurry through the grasses. May it be a busy place for all the little creatures that sip and nibble and munch among the flowers. May it be a joyful place for all the birds that sing in the trees.

Freedom

We share the earth
we share the sky
we share the shining sea
with those we trust
with those we fear:
we are God's family.

O God,
May each and every one of us have space
    to grow to be our true selves.
May we find space for ourselves.
May we allow space for others.

I pray for those who are trapped:
in prison, in fear, in poverty.

They want to dance for the joy of dancing.
They want to sing for the joy of singing.
They want to laugh for the joy of laughing.

O God, unlock the door that holds them in misery.

Justice

Heal the world's sorrows
Dry the world's tears
Calm the world's worries
End the world's fears.

There's trouble in the fields, Lord,
The crops are parched and dry.
We water them with tears, Lord,
So help us, hear our cry.

There's trouble in our hearts, Lord,
The world is full of pain.
Set us to work for healing,
Send blessings down like rain.

O God,
We remember those who have no house
  to call their home.
Give them shelter.

We remember those who have no country
  to call their home.
Give them refuge.

May we remember that we belong
  to the world's great family
and find a way to help them,
  our brothers and sisters.

Peace

❧

O God,
Settle the quarrels among the nations.

May they hammer their swords into ploughs and their
spears into pruning knives…

Where the tanks now roll, let there be tractors;
where the landmines explode, let the fields grow crops.

Let there be a harvest of fruit and grain
and peace that all the world can share.

Based on Micah 4:3–5

Dear God,
Give us the courage to overcome anger with love.

We pray for the children
Who were born to know war,
Who were born to know grief,
Who were born to know violence.

May they learn gentleness,
May they learn joy,
May they learn peace.

Praying as Jesus taught

Jesus was a Jew. As a boy, he learned about his Jewish faith. Part of that was saying prayers to God.

When Jesus became a preacher, he still got up early to say his prayers. Often, he went out into the countryside where he could be alone with God.

'When you pray,' said Jesus to his followers, 'don't be like the hypocrites. They love to stand up and pray where everyone will see them.

'Instead, when you pray, go to your room, close the door and pray to your Father, who is unseen. And your Father, who sees what you do in private, will reward you.'

Jesus welcomed children as equal members of God's family.

72

Jesus criticized people who showed off about how much they prayed.

Jesus told people to pray alone and quietly.

God will take care of those who trust in him, as a good shepherd takes care of his sheep.

The prayer Jesus taught

~

'When you pray,' said Jesus to his followers, 'do not
use a lot of meaningless words… Your Father already
knows what you need before you ask him. This, then,
is how you should pray:

'Our Father in heaven,
hallowed be your name,
your kingdom come,
your will be done,
on earth as in heaven.
Give us today our daily bread.
Forgive us our sins
as we forgive those who sin against us.
Lead us not into temptation
but deliver us from evil.

'For the kingdom, the power,
and the glory are yours
now and for ever.
Amen.'

The Lord's Prayer, with a traditional ending

God's love and care

Jesus said:
Ask, and you will receive;
seek, and you will find;
knock, and the door will be opened to you.

For everyone who asks will receive,
and anyone who seeks will find,
and the door will be opened to those who knock.

Your Father in heaven will give good things
to those who ask him.

From Matthew 7:7–8, 11

God feeds the birds that sing from the treetops;
God feeds the birds that wade by the sea;
God feeds the birds that dart through the meadows;
So will God take care of me?

God clothes the flowers that bloom on the hillside;
God clothes the blossom that hangs from the tree;
As God cares so much for the birds and the flowers
I know God will take care of me.

A prayer based on Jesus' Sermon on the Mount, Matthew 6

The kingdom of God

❧

Jesus called the children to him and said, 'Let the children come to me and do not stop them, because the kingdom of God belongs to such as these.'

Luke 18:16

The kingdom of God
is like a tree
growing through all eternity.

In its branches, birds may nest;
in its shade we all may rest.

*A prayer inspired by Jesus' parable of the
mustard seed, Matthew 13*

Dear God,
I am your lost sheep.
Please find me.
Please take me home.

The right way

Dear God,
Help me to find the right way to go,
even though the gate to it be narrow,
and the path difficult to walk.

Based on Matthew 7:13

O God,
Save me from collecting a mountain of possessions
that weigh me down on this earth
and that will crumble away here.

Instead, help me to travel lightly along the way of
righteousness
expecting no reward for what I do
but confident of riches in heaven.

A prayer inspired by Jesus' teaching, Luke 12:33–34

I resolve this day
to follow Jesus
in all I do.

I resolve each day
to follow Jesus
in all I do.

Then the work of all my days
will be like a house built on rock
that is safe in God's care
for ever.

Based on Matthew 7:24–25

Loving others

֍

Lord God,
Help me to love you with all my heart, with all
my soul, and with all my mind.

Help me to love other people as much as myself.

Based on Jesus' words about the commandments,
Matthew 22:37–40

Dear God,
Help me to love my enemies.
Show me how to do good things
for those who hurt me.
Remind me to pray for those
who are unkind.

Based on Luke 6:27–28

Lord Jesus,
You told us to love one another.
May I be eager to help others.
May I not think myself more important
    than them.
May I follow your example of being
    humble and hardworking.

Based on John 13

Blessings

The Bible says that God will bless those who live in the way that is good and right.

There may be hard times. Sometimes unkind people will do well. Sometimes bad things will happen.

But God's love and mercy are unending. They are as sure as the sunrise. People can trust in God's blessing.

God's people will help one another and anyone in need.

God has promised to take care of people in good times and in bad.

God blesses everyone each day with a world that can provide for them.

Asking God's blessing

May the Lord bless you.
May the Lord take care of you.
May the light of his goodness
always shine upon you.
May you enjoy good things.
May you live in peace.

From Numbers 6:24–26

Wherever you go,
May God the Father be with you.
Wherever you go,
May God the Son be with you.
Wherever you go,
May God the Spirit be with you.

Bless the dawn and bless the sun:
Bless the morning just begun.

Bless the light and bless the day:
Bless us in our work and play.

Bless the earth and bless the sea:
God bless you and God bless me.

For loved ones

God bless those who are dear to me,
God bless those who are near to me;
God bless those who are far away,
God bless all of us through the day.

God bless you who are here on my left,
And God bless you on my right;
May God keep you safe all through the day
And guard you all through the night.

A circle blessing

God bless all those that I love;
God bless all those that love me;
God bless all those that love those that I love,
And all those that love those that love me.

From an old New England sampler

For goodbyes

May the road rise to meet you.
May the wind be always at your back.
May the sun shine warm upon your face,
the rains fall soft upon your fields and,
until we meet again,
may God hold you in the palm of his hand.

Irish blessing

Deep peace of the running waves to you,
Deep peace of the flowing air to you,
Deep peace of the quiet earth to you,
Deep peace of the shining stars to you,
Deep peace of the shades of night to you,
Moon and stars always giving light to you,
Deep peace of Christ, the Son of Peace, to you.

Traditional Gaelic blessing

For the night-time

Guardian angel, stay close by
while the moon floats through the sky.

Bless the thoughts that fill my head
while I lie awake in bed.

Bless the way my body curls
as the sail of dreams unfurls.

Guardian angel, stay close by
while the moon floats through the sky.

Bless the day, dear God, from sunrise to sunset.
Bless the night, dear God, from sunset to sunrise.

When I lie down, I go to sleep in peace;
you alone, O Lord, keep me perfectly safe.

Psalm 4:8

Index of first lines